The History of Postal Services from 6,000 Years Ago to the Present

The Earliest Known Writing
Is Still Undecipherable

Tom Riley

HERITAGE BOOKS
2018

HERITAGE BOOKS

AN IMPRINT OF HERITAGE BOOKS, INC.

Books, CDs, and more—Worldwide

For our listing of thousands of titles see our website
at
www.HeritageBooks.com

Published 2018 by
HERITAGE BOOKS, INC.
Publishing Division
5810 Ruatan Street
Berwyn Heights, Md. 20740

International Standard Book Numbers
Paperbound: 978-0-7884-5818-7

This book is dedicated to my wonderful wife, Crucy, I love you. It is also dedicated to my daughters, Dr. Bernadette Ann Riley and Dr. Gina Maria Riley, you are my inspiration; and, the finest classical guitarist, composer and author I know, Benjamin Noah Riley. It is also dedicated to the great team at Heritage Books, Inc.: president and owner, Craig Scott; publishing director, Leslie Wolfinger; and most of all, my editor, Debbie Riley, whose kind words, thoughtful suggestions and illustrations made all the difference.

CHAPTER I

Early Communication Systems

The need for a system to exchange written communication has been felt by all societies. This very basic need to communicate over a long distance marks the advent of postal services. Communication, the lifeblood of every society has undergone tremendous advances over the centuries. One of the earliest messages as recorded in the Old Testament of the Bible was transported by a dove to Noah in the form of an olive branch. Moses inscribed the Ten Commandments in stone tablets to stress their importance and to etch into the memory of his people lasting principles of human conduct.

From these etchings into a stone tablet to the transfer of electronic mail via satellites a long difficult process has taken place. As speedier means of transporting letters were devised so did the demand for postal services increase.

The basic function of postal organizations is to turn that letter that you mail and place in a collection box into something that can be handled on a bulk basis, so that eventually it can regain its individual status.

Good communication was essential for governing the vast empires of the ancient world. The Egyptians had a unique way of transmitting messages. Around 4,000 B.C. the Pharaoh wanted to transmit a message to a general fighting a battle hundreds of miles away. He called in his servant and had his head shaved and inscribed a message on his bald head. He held him in captivity until his hair grew back. He was then sent on his way. If he became apprehended he could rightly claim no knowledge of the message. The intended receiver of the message would shave the servant's head to read the Pharaoh's decrees. Many centuries later papyrus was used for extensive record-keeping and messages because of its light weight.

Around 3,500 B.C. in the Persian Gulf Region, the King pressed his ring into a clay tablet where a message had been inscribed. The tablet was set out in the hot desert sun to dry. Once dried, mounted couriers delivered these heavy letters. A treasure trove of these heavy letters was discovered in the early 1900s in a cave in Turkey. They offer a vivid account of business transactions and court life of that era.

The Chinese developed a Post House Relay System that is credited as the world's first Postal Service. Under the Chou Dynasty (1,000 B.C.) mounted couriers delivered messages on paper, which was invented by the Chinese. These couriers delivered the Emperor's decrees to far-flung villages and provinces. The postal service was not for public use and anyone caught using it for their own use did so under the penalty of death. The relay system was brought to a high state of development under the Mongol Emperors. In the 13th century Marco Polo remarked that the Post House relay system reached every corner of the Empire with over 25,000 stations.

The Chinese used three classes of mail. Herodotus, the Greek historian described his admiration for the Post House Relay System of Cyrus the Great of Persia in the 6th century B.C. Those words are etched into the facade of the Manhattan General Post office on 34th Street. "Neither snow, nor rain, nor gloom of night shall stop these carriers from the full completion of their appointed rounds."

These words come to the minds of New Yorkers as they see mail carriers enter their shops to deliver mail in all kinds of weather. Herodotus's words are as timely today as they were twenty-five hundred years ago.

It was the development of Rome from a small city state into a vast Empire that ushered in the most highly developed postal system in the world. The Roman Empire with its ability to construct a vast network of roads to unite its far-flung provinces created in turn a need to communicate with them. The Roman Cursus Publicus or Roman Post Office was established at convenient intervals along the great roads of the Empire. The Cursus Publicus served the political and military needs of the Empire for a speedy and reliable system of communication between Rome and its many provinces.

Chariots were used to carry the mail, often holding over 400 pounds of letters.

An inspectorial system to oversee the operation and prevent abuses was similar in nature to our own Postal Inspection Service. The Cursus Publicus was highly organized and the speed at which it could deliver messages was not to be rivaled until the 19th century.

After the fall of the Roman Empire in the west, the political fragmentation of Europe caused all traces of the Roman Postal System to disappear. Although the barbarian rulers admired the Cursus Publicis and tried to keep it intact, communities bordering the great roads refused to maintain them and they fell into disarray. The lack of central administration in Rome and the political disintegration of the times broke apart the Cursus Publicus.

In the Americas, the pre-Columbian civilization felt the same need to communicate. The Mayans developed a road network for foot messengers that lasted 1,000 years. The Incas also developed means to communicate over long distances by relay systems. American Indians developed a rudimentary parcel post system to transfer fresh catches of fish and game to their villages by means of foot messengers.

CHAPTER II

Pigeons, Kites and Camels

The ingenuity of man in devising means to communicate over long distance is a tribute to man's imagination. He has at various times used: reindeers, zinc-coated steel balls, camels, sea currents and horses.

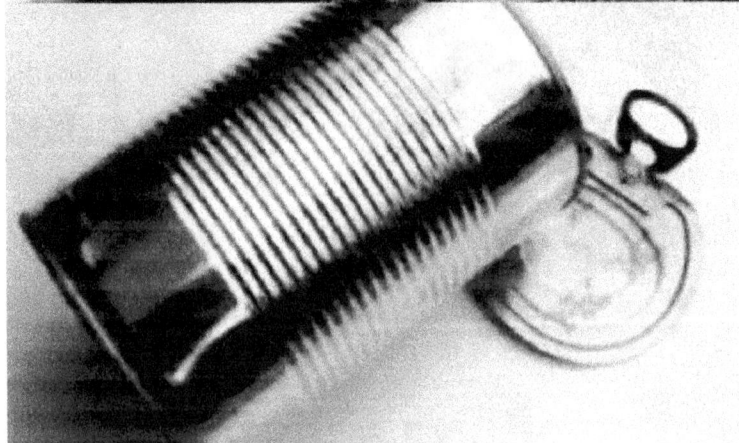

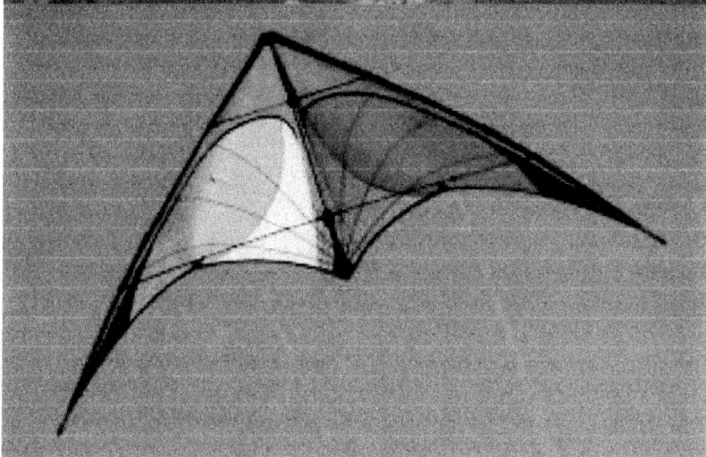

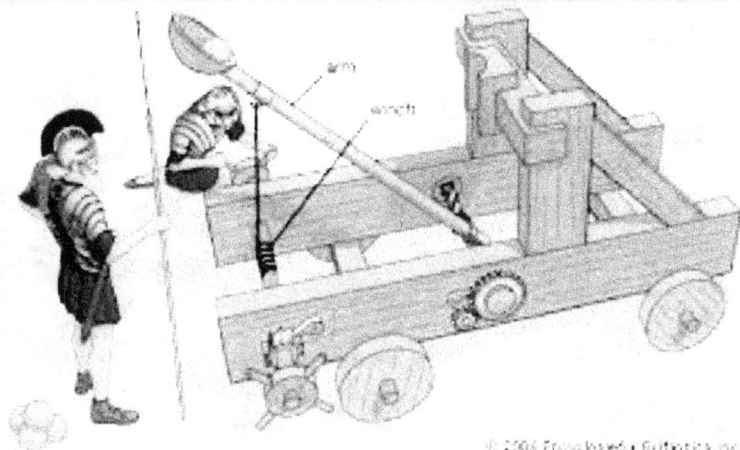

© 2006 Encyclopædia Britannica, Inc.

As faster means of communication were devised the postal service was quick to make use of them. Electronic mail delivery using satellites to aid delivery and drones are the most modern examples of the quest to communicate as rapidly as possible.

Mail has fostered the bonds of friendship and opened doors to new opportunities for millions of people. The immigrant to Africa is connected to his native country by the bonds of weekly correspondence with family back home. Business opportunities are spotted and relayed so commerce is enlarged between countries. The expansion of the European Economic Community results in greater correspondence and increased demand for postal services.

Information is power and the transmission of mail throughout the global community will improve as the 21st century unfolds.

The Greek philosopher, Theophrastus launched bottles containing messages into the Mediterranean. He wanted to prove that the Mediterranean fed into the Atlantic Ocean. Sea Currents took his bottles into the Atlantic where mariners recovered his bottles and proved his theory. Probably the first airborne letter was sent on an arrow during a siege of an embattlement long before the birth of Christ.

We know the first airborne message to man was sent to Noah by a dove bearing an olive branch. That message of hope to a besieged humanity proved God's love for all living things.

Pigeons have a long history in aiding man in his desire to communicate. Ancient Greeks, Hebrews, Chinese and Persians often used pigeons during sieges. Pigeons wounded in flight have been known to walk home. With the development of microfilm the importance of pigeons magnified. During a siege of Paris in 1871 microfilm was inserted into goose quills that were tied to the pigeon's tail feathers. Over 30,000 letters could be sent this way on one pigeon.

The Chinese used kites to transport messages during a siege in the 6th century A.D. The English used balloons in the late 1700s to drop letters overboard. As faster, more efficient means of transportation were devised so man used it to communicate. Dogs, cats, camels and reindeer were used at various times until technology improved to the point where steamships, railroads and airplanes aided communication. Now computers, satellites and fax machines provide even faster means to communicate.

It was during the industrial revolution that the demand for better mail service to serve the growing commercial and manufacturing centers took place. The improved roads of London and the development of the stagecoach speeded up delivery of mail. Letters could be delivered the morning after posting in towns 120 miles from London.

In 1837, a British educator and tax reformer, Rowland Hill published *Post Office Reform: Its Importance and Practicability*. It is regarded as a milestone in postal progress. He studied the cost structure of postal operations and came to the conclusion that conveyance charges were not an important factor in the total cost of mailing a letter. He realized the current intricate charging scales based on distances were irrelevant. He also showed how the collection of money payment was easily avoidable. Hill's solution was a uniform rate of postage regardless of distance using prepaid adhesive stamps sold by the post office.

Hill's proposal gained strong support. His one penny for each half ounce of mail found favor with the general public. The "Penny Post" was introduced in 1840 and was an instant success because it brought postal services to the masses.

Today, the modern postal service is indebted to Hill's reforms. They are the key to the speed and delivery with which the modern postal system handles billions of letters daily. The reduced rate of postage for printed matter helped the spread of education.

The development of the railroad speeded up the delivery of mail. Letters were sorted in transit and delivered the day after at distances three to four times as great as had been possible by stagecoach. By the end of the 19th century, Britain, France, the U.S. and India had built up a complex network of rail service.

INTERNATIONAL POSTAL REFORM

Postal relations between countries were composed of a bewildering variety of currencies and units of weight and measurements. Postal treaties worked out between countries became so complex that they interfered with the free exchange of international mail. Something had to be done.

The first practical steps toward reform took place in May 1863 when delegates of fifteen European and American postal administrations met at the Paris Postal Conference which was convened at the suggestion of the United States. The conference established important general principles for the simplification of procedures, which were adopted as a model by the countries concerned.

The American Civil War delayed a formal international treaty. On September 15th the International Postal Congress met in Bern, Switzerland. It was attended by representatives of twenty-two states. On October 9th, 1874 a "Treaty Concerning the Establishment of a General Postal Union" was signed. The treaty provided a uniform framework of rules and procedures for the exchanges of international mail. The Union grew rapidly to 140 countries. By 1914 when China was admitted it included almost all independent countries. Since 1948 the U.P.U. has been a specialized agency of the United Nations.

Postal Services today still rely on carriers and clerks to mediate the delivery of mail. The use of automation and optical scanners keep the price of mailing a letter cost-effective. In 1875 it cost $5.00 to mail a letter from Missouri to San Francisco via Pony Express. Today it costs only forty-six cents to mail a letter that distance. The postal service in the U.S. is still the most cost effective in terms of mail delivery among the industrialized countries of the world.

CHAPTER III

The U.S. Postal Service: From Benjamin Franklin to Air Mail

The "father of the U.S. Postal Service" Benjamin Franklin was appointed Postmaster General of the United States by the Second Continental Congress on July 26, 1775. His postal achievements were a small part of the contributions this man made to the era. His accomplishments as a printer, publisher, philosopher, philanthropist and statesman made him a legend even in his own time. He received a salary of $1,000 a year.

Before that, the English Crown had appointed him Postmaster General of Philadelphia in 1727. Franklin made many improvements. Surveys were made and shorter routes drawn up. He reported his first surplus to the British Crown.

He improved postal operations from Maine to Florida and mail operated on a regular schedule. While Postmaster Franklin formed the first Volunteer Fire Department, he also started America's first hospital and started an academy that later became the University of Pennsylvania. As an inventor Franklin had few peers. He invented bi-focal glasses, the lightning rod, copper plates to make money and the Franklin stove. Franklin became associated with changes that have had a lasting impact on the postal system. He designed distribution cases containing pigeon holes for the deposit of mail for common destinations. He also improved the post roads by setting milestones (stone markers) along the roads. He also established the Postal Inspection Service. When Franklin died in 1790 in Philadelphia he was accorded one of the largest funerals the city had ever seen.

Passage of the Act of 1837 made all railroads in the U.S. post routes. Mail intended for local points was sorted and dropped off at local stops. By 1930 10,000 were being used to deliver mail to every hamlet in the U.S. By 1970 virtually all railroads were eliminated as mail transporters.

During the Civil War street boxes began to appear for mail collection. Free City Delivery was instituted in 1863. Postmaster Montgomery Blair served under President Lincoln. Blair had to meet unprecedented demand for postal services. Blair worked out a plan which gave every regiment its own postmaster. He reduced the deficit in the Post Office from $5.7 million to a surplus of $161,000 when he retired.

In 1889 President Benjamin Harrison appointed John Wanamaker Postmaster General. Wanamaker was a Philadelphia merchant and a marketing genius. He believed the Post Office should be operated as a business-just as his store was. He emphasized a postal building program and services to the customer. He initiated house letter boxes, free delivery, parcel post and postal savings.

By 1880, 454 post offices were delivering mail to residents of U.S. cities. It was in 1900 that free delivery came to farmers and other rural residents. Before that people had to go to the post office to pick up their mail. If they refused a letter the post office labor and delivery cost were never recovered.

It is difficult for us to imagine the isolation and loneliness of the American farmer. One farmer estimated he travelled 12,000 miles going to and from the post office to get the mail. Some farmers got together and paid $2,600 to pave the road so they could get rural free delivery.

When Parcel Post became law the Sears and Roebucks Catalogue was considered the "homesteaders Bible" and Sears and Roebuck tripled it business.

AIRMAIL

The U.S. government was slow to recognize the importance of the airplane, but the Post Office was intrigued with the possibility of carrying mail through the skies. It authorized experimental mail flights. Earl Ovington dropped mail over Mineola, Long Island and the postmaster retrieved it. Within three months the U.S. mail was flown both day and night from San Francisco to New York.

These early planes had no instruments, radios or other navigation aids. Pilots flew by dead reckoning or by "the seat of their pants." Fatalities were rare because of the slow landing speed of the planes. By 1926 commercial airlines took over air mail delivery.

CHAPTER IV

⟨he ⟨Pony ⟨Express

The Pony Express is memorable to adults and children alike because it romanticized the rough and tumble days of the settling of the American West. Rowe Findley wrote an article in the July 1980 National Geographic magazine that tells the story of that era.

"Here he Comes!"

Away across the endless dead level of the prairie a black speck appears against the sky ... sweeping toward us nearer and nearer ... a whoop and a wave of the hand ... and the man and his horse burst past our view and goes winging into the distance."

Mark Twain from a westbound stage beheld a Pony Express rider and so the rider has galloped into history, hat brim bent by the wind, dust flying from the staccato beat of dust digging hoofbeats. The pony express looms larger than truth, a buckaroo stew of fact and legend. The pony express rider risked death daily as Indian wars flamed across hundreds of miles of Utah territory, destroying relay stations, stock and seventeen lives, including one to three riders depending on whose facts you accept. The bravest death is attributed to an orphan, age fourteen.

William F. Cody earned his spurs as a pony express rider at fifteen. He earned the nickname "Wild Bill" in a controversial shoot-out while in the employ of the Pony Express. Another spunky lad, Elijah "Nick" Wilson survived a barbed arrow in his skull and so inspired dime store novelist Ned Buntline, who wrote about his hair-raising adventures.

The true facts are that the pony express rider averaged ten miles an hour. In darkness or uphill he slowed for safety or to spare his mount and he usually arrived on time with the mail and scalp intact. The Pony Express lasted only eighteen months and grew out of a long-frustrated need. By 1860 almost half a million Americans lived west of the

Rocky Mountain, most of them in California and Oregon. They were lured there by the opportunity for land and gold and they were concerned about news from home, those settled states, east of the Missouri River.

The freighting firm of Russell, Majors and Wadell already possessed of fifty-five acres of corralled horses decided they had a head start as they already were running a stage line to all U.S. Army posts in the West. Most of the horses were western mustangs, good for fast getaways from Indians.

The Pony Express began in St. Joseph, Missouri, the western end of the nation's railroads in 1860 and ended at Sacramento quay where the mail was flung aboard a side steamer for San Francisco. Several months after it began the Paiutes, numbering perhaps 8,000 men, rose in holy war to chase the white man from what is today most of Nevada and a slice of Utah. War parties attacked ranches and many Pony

Express Stations came under attack. Seventeen employees were killed. One rider, Nick Wilson remembered fighting off the Indians for three days. He was struck just above the eye. His friends pulled the arrow out but the flint spike remained embedded in his skull. His friends thought he was a goner. They abandoned him but came back the next day to bury him. They found him still alive. He remained in a coma for eighteen days but recovered.

Billy Tate, fourteen, an orphan train rider who signed on to ride for the Pony Express was carrying the mail near Ruby Valley when a dozen braves rode him down in a desperate stand behind a rock. Friends later found him, pierced by many arrows, with seven of his attackers dead before him. The slain Billy still had his scalp, a sign that the warriors respected his courage.

Bill Cody, fatherless with a mother and sister in need, hired on as a Pony Express rider at fifteen. Cody once rode 322 miles to deliver the mail when several riders were killed by Indians.

It was the telegraph that put the Pony Express out of business. The telegraph project was a race by crews building east and west to see who could get to Salt Lake City first. The Missouri crew under Edward Creighton got there October 18th, 1861, the Californians under James Gamble six days later. The first message eastward assured President Lincoln of California's loyalty to the Union. In mere minutes it dot-dashed across the same route the Pony Express had ridden. In eighteen and a half months, by most estimates the enterprise lost $200,000.

CHAPTER V

The U.S. Postal Service Undergoes Era of Change

The following information is excerpted from the *History of the U.S. Postal Service 1775-1984* by Rita L. Moroney, Research Administrator/Historian.

The social correspondence of the earlier century gave way, gradually at first, then explosively, to business mail, until in 1963 business mail constituted 80% of the total volume. The largest impetus to this great outpouring was the result of the computer. Something had to be done. The introduction of the Zip Code and the development of 552 sectional centers, each serving 40 to 150 post offices allowed the post office to handle the record volume.

In 1966 the Chicago Post Office grounded to a virtual stop under a log jam of mail. The case for Postal Reform was summarized by Postmaster General Lawrence F. O'Brian. "We have no control over our work load, over the rates and revenue, over the pay rates for employees, over the conditions of the service of these employees and limited control over the transportation facilities we are compelled to use."

WORKERS RISK IT ALL IN HISTORIC STRIKE

On March 17th, 1970 The National Association of Letter Carriers went on strike, touching off the largest wildcat strike in U.S. history and the only one in postal history.

New York Post

NEW YORK, THURSDAY, MARCH 19, 1970

CITY HARD HIT BY MAIL STRIKE

The strikers stayed out even under the threat of fines, jail sentences and losing their jobs. "It changed everything" said Thomas Germano, one of the strikers and now director of the Cornell University Industrial Relations Department. "More changed in eight days than in 200 years prior to that —certainly more rapid and lasting changes." When it was over, President Nixon signed the Postal Reorganization Act of 1970 which made the Postal Service an independent establishment within the executive branch of the government. The major accomplishments under Reorganization include:

A) Streamline the Management
B) Abolished patronage
C) Started Express Mail
0) Computerized Forwarding
E) Offered First Class Discounts
F) Consumer Advocate for Complaints
G) Use Color Labels to reduce Misrouting
H) Accept Passport Applications
I) Keep Rates the Lowest in the Industrialized World
J) Devised Carrier Alert Program
K) Modernized the Physical Plants

L) Increase in Productivity
M) Cracked down on Postal Violators
N) Purchased Fuel Efficient Vehicles
O) Raised Employees wages
P) Offered Automated Windows
Q) Instituted Energy Efficiency
R) Streamlined insurance Claims and
many more innovations.

CHAPTER VI

Stamp Collecting

The following Chapter contains information excerpted from *Stories Behind the Stamps* by Doug Storer. "The Soliloquy of a Postage Stamp" was also borrowed from that fine book.

Soliloquy of a Postage Stamp

I am the world's greatest traveler. I have journeyed from pole to pole and all the climes between ... by dogsled, camel and horseback, by every sea and air conveyance, even by submarine, dirigible and rocket.

I am the world's greatest art and portrait gallery. The heroes and heroines of mythology pose within my borders. I portray greats and near greats of all times; Kings and Queens, Pharaohs and presidents, princes and princesses, poets and patriots, emperors and explorers, athletes, architects, aviators, artists and adventurers, tribal chiefs, inventors, dramatists and novelists, shahs, sultans, saints and sinners. Even the vanished forms of the phoenix, dragon, centaur and unicorn appear upon my face.

I am the world's greatest picture chronicle and miniature encyclopedia. I map communities, countries and continents, and reveal views from every strange remote corner of the earth. I depict mountains and valleys, monuments, temples and ruins of temples; and every type of locomotion from automobiles to zeppelins and steamboats to space ships. I delineate all matter of sports, handicraft, customs, sacred rites and ceremonies; and nearly every variety of bird, fish, animal, fruit and flower.

I frame the horrors of war, the blessings of peace, the hardships of emigration, the plight of indigence and the blight of famine. I illustrate the adventures of Don Quixote, the fairytale of childhood and the legends of all civilizations. I reflect the symbols of art and culture, of natural resources and industry, of trade and commerce, of agriculture and architecture, and of all human endeavor. I commemorate the expeditions and voyages, and the inventions, discoveries and creations that make life worth living.

Millions of men, women and children are fascinated by me. Through my infinite variety they find boundless pleasure, relaxation and enchantment.

Yet ... I am only a postage stamp!

One of the most avid stamp collectors had this to say about his hobby: "One of the best things about stamp collecting is that the enthusiasm which it arouses in youth increases as the years pass. It dispels boredom, enlarges our vision, broadens our knowledge and in innumerable ways enriches our life. I also commend stamp collecting because I really believe it makes one a better citizen." This is how Franklin Delano Roosevelt felt about his hobby, stamp collecting.

CHAPTER VII

Rare Stamps:
The Twenty-Four Cent Air Mail Invert

A man named W. T. Robey walked into his local post office to buy a sheet of the just-issued twenty-four cent U.S. Air Mail stamps. He put down his $24.00 dollars and received 100 stamps from the postal clerk. As Robey turned from the window, he glanced down at the stamps in his hands. Then he stopped and looked at them again, all the pictures of the planes were upside down! As an amateur collector, Mr. Robey knew he had a great find, what philatelists call an "inverted center." Most of these errors never make it to the post office. They are found and destroyed by sharp-eyed government checkers before the stamps leave the printing plant.

To make certain it was a great find, he went back to the postal clerk and asked if other sheets showed the plane inverted. There were none. A check of other post offices showed Mr. Robey owned the only sheet like it in the world.

Mr. Robey sold these 100 "inverts" to Eugene Klein of Philadelphia in 1918. Mr. Klein paid him $15,000 for the $24.00 sheet. The sheet was later broken up and sold to collectors. The last price listed for one of the "24 cent Air Mail Inverts" is a stunning $500,000.

THE TWO CENT HAWAIIAN POSTAGE STAMP

In June of 1892 a well-known stamp collector named Gaston Leroux was found murdered in his Paris apartment. The police were puzzled by the crime as Leroux had no enemies and nothing seemed to have been stolen. A sharp-eyed detective with an interest in philately noticed that a rare "Hawaiian Missionaries" stamp had disappeared from the dead man's famous collection.

Shortly afterwards, the missing stamp turned up in the collection of another Paris philatelist who had been a friend of Leroux. The man later confessed he had strangled Leroux in a fit of anger after her refused to sell him the stamp.

The group of valuable stamps known as "Hawaiian Missionaries" takes its name from the fact that most of them were found on letters sent from Hawaii by missionaries who had gone to the Islands from the United States during the mid-1800's.

The value of "the Dawson Cover" on which two Hawaiian stamps were placed was $2,100,000.

This cover was last sold for $2,100,000.

The Dawson Cover was retrieved from a furnace thirty-five years after it was burned. It was packed tightly and shows slight evidence of burning on the left.

Postage stamps were first issued in Hawaii in 1851. Not many stamps were issued as there was only a limited demand for them as most Hawaiians of that period did not know how to write.

THE BRITISH GUIANA

In 1873 a young English schoolboy was spending a rainy afternoon rummaging through some faded letters kept by his family in an attic. He was looking for some old stamps that might find a place in his album. He found a very dirty and crudely printed stamp but decided not to keep it, so he sold it to a young friend who also collected stamps. He couldn't know it then, of course, that he had just sold what was to become the world's rarest, most valuable bit of old paper for $1.50.

It was the 1 cent black on magenta "British Guiana" stamp which had been issued in 1856 when that little South American country was a colony of the Crown.

The stamp was later sold to a dealer in Scotland, who thought it was a curiosity. He later sold it to Count Ferrary, at the time the world's greatest stamp collector, for the sum of $750.00. The Count kept it in his collection for over forty years, during which time it was established as being the only stamp of its kind in the whole world.

After Ferrary's death in 1917 the "British Guiana" was sold to a wealthy American, Arthur Hind, who paid $38,000 for the world famous rarity. When Hind died his executors were surprised to see no "British Guiana" in his collection. He had given it to his wife as a present and she wisely had put it in the vault of a New York bank. The "British Guiana" has changed hands only once since that time and today the old stamp which a boy sold to his friend for $1.50 is now valued at over $10,000,000.

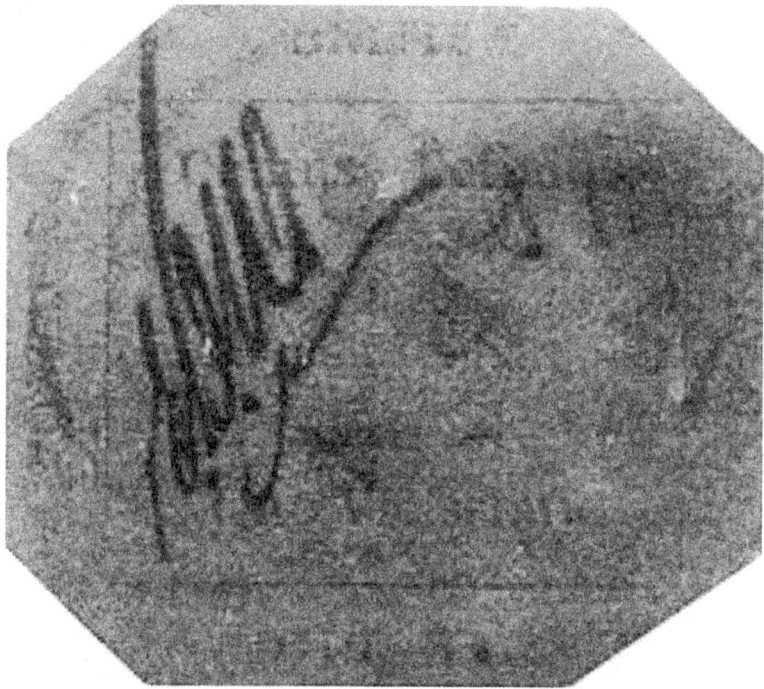

Heritage Books by the author:

Andrew Horace Burke
A Man for All Seasons: The Incredible Story of an Orphan Train Rider
and Civil War Drummer Boy Who Grew Up to Become
the Governor of North Dakota

Happy Valley School: A History and Remembrance

Orphan Train Riders: A Brief History of the Orphan Train Era (1854–1929)
with Entrance Records from the American Female Guardian
Society's Home for the Friendless in New York
Volume One

Orphan Train Riders: Entrance Records from the
American Female Guardian Society's Home
for the Friendless in New York
Volume Two

The Big Green Book: How the Environmental Decisions We Make in
These Turbulent Economic Times Will Effect America and the World

The History of Postal Services from 6,000 Years Ago to the Present:
The Earliest Known Writing Is Still Undecipherable

The Orphan Train to Destiny

The Stuyvesant Connection

We Deliver: A Chronicle of the Deeds Performed by the
Men and Women of the U.S. Postal Service

www.ingramcontent.com/pod-product-compliance
Lightning Source LLC
Chambersburg PA
CBHW052108270326
41931CB00012B/2937